Basher

123

Basher

123

KINGFISHER
NEW YORK

One

One smiling snake
cuddles his favorite teddy bear.

Two

1 2 3 4 5 6 7 8 9 10 11 12 13 14 15 16 17 18 19 20

Two mischievous monkeys
play tennis in the rain.

Three

1 2 <u>3</u> 4 5 6 7 8 9 10 11 12 13 14 15 16 17 18 19 20

Three messy pigs
bake tiny cupcakes.

Four

Four freaky frogs
have holes in their socks.

Five

1 2 3 4 <u>5</u> 6 7 8 9 10 11 12 13 14 15 16 17 18 19 20

Five smart caterpillars
blow shiny pink bubbles.

Six

Six greedy penguins
gobble juicy jelly beans.

Seven

1 2 3 4 5 6 <u>7</u> 8 9 10 11 12 13 14 15 16 17 18 19 20

Seven tiny rabbits
jump around in cowboy hats.

Eight

Eight sad mice
lose their red balloon.

Nine

Nine daring ladybugs
show off on their skateboards.

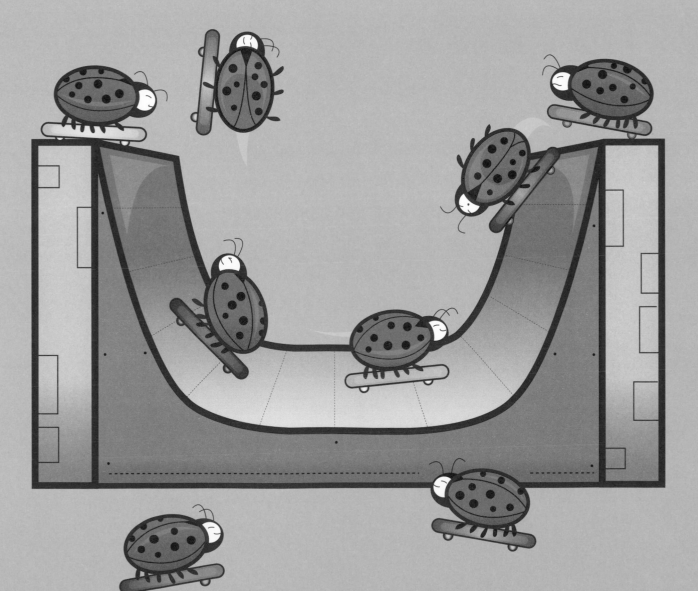

Ten

Ten giggly cows
whirl Hula-Hoops on their hips.

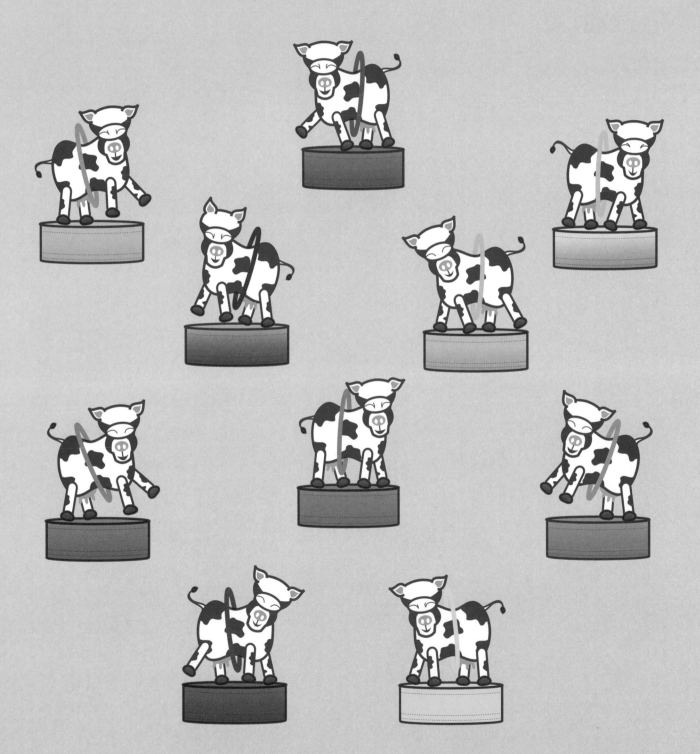

Eleven

1 2 3 4 5 6 7 8 9 10 11 12 13 14 15 16 17 18 19 20

Eleven glamorous butterflies wear sparkly sunglasses.

Twelve

1 2 3 4 5 6 7 8 9 10 11 <u>12</u> 13 14 15 16 17 18 19 20

Twelve twinkling stars
wave a bright hello to Earth.

Thirteen

Thirteen speedy snails
rev up their red racecars.

Fourteen

Fourteen fearless kites
fly higher and higher.

Fifteen

Fifteen angry ants
cool off by the pool.

Sixteen

Sixteen lost clouds find their way home.

Seventeen

Seventeen hungry flies
take a lollipop home for dinner.

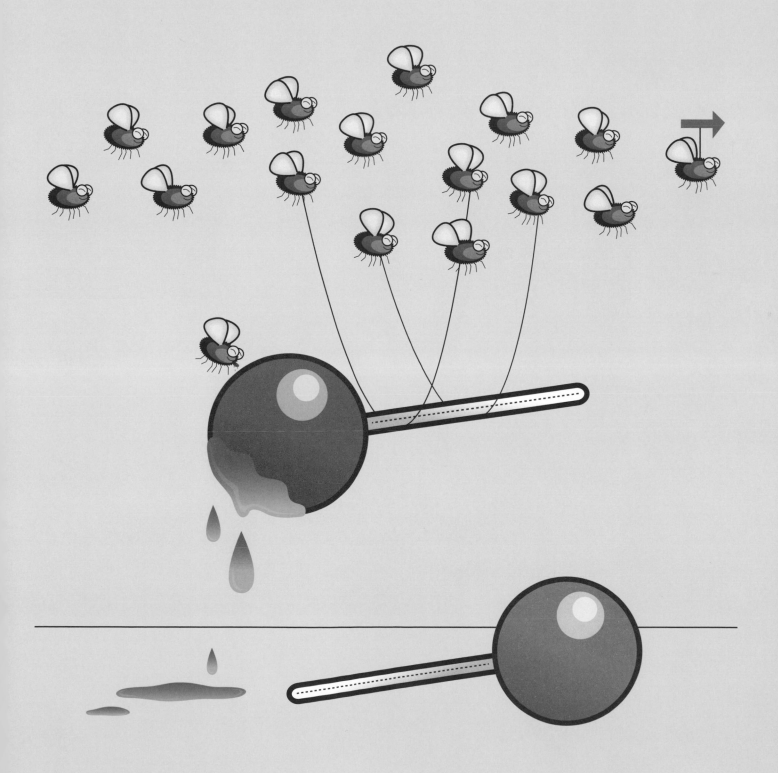

Eighteen

Eighteen baby elephants toot trumpets in a band.

Nineteen

1 2 3 4 5 6 7 8 9 10 11 12 13 14 15 16 17 18 <u>19</u> 20

Nineteen naughty sheep
splash and jump in puddles.

Twenty

1 2 3 4 5 6 7 8 9 10 11 12 13 14 15 16 17 18 19 <u>20</u>

Twenty sleepy spiders
whisper goodnight.

KINGFISHER
LONDON & NEW YORK

Copyright © Simon Basher 2012
Published in the United States by Kingfisher,
175 Fifth Ave., New York, NY 10010
Kingfisher is an imprint of Macmillan Children's Books, London.
All rights reserved.

Designed and created by Basher www.basherbooks.com

Dedicated to the Master Chickens: Kas, Jos & Ella.

Distributed in the U.S. and Canada by Macmillan,
175 Fifth Ave., New York, NY 10010

Library of Congress Cataloging-in-Publication data has been applied for.

ISBN: 978-0-7534-6772-5

Kingfisher books are available for special promotions and premiums.
For details contact: Special Markets Department, Macmillan,
175 Fifth Ave., New York, NY 10010.

For more information, please visit www.kingfisherbooks.com

Printed in China
1 3 5 7 9 8 6 4 2
1TR/0312/WKT/UNTD/140WFO